Chambering for Ackley Cartridges

Gunsmithing Student Handbook Series

#1

By Fred Zeglin

Chambering for Ackley Cartridges

Copyright© 2014, Fred Zeglin

ISBN# 978-0-9831598-3-4

Library of Congress# 2014954764

Published by
4D Reamer Rentals LTD
432 E. Idaho St., Suite C420
Kalispell, MT 59901

Foreword

When I first became aware of Fred Zeglin's proposed "Gunsmithing Student Handbook Series", I was more than pleased. This series of textbooks on the gunsmithing arts and sciences is long overdue and promises to be invaluable to both on campus and distance learning students. When finished, it will provide a common core of knowledge on the various every day gunsmithing tasks. As things stand now, each residence school has its own method of teaching and a myriad of instructors, each teaching "The One True Method" as they learned it from other instructors or experience. This results in a very uneven product in their graduating students. If used by enough of the half dozen or so residence schools around the country and working gunsmiths, it can establish a baseline for the way many common jobs should be done.

As an example, this first volume covers "Chambering for Ackley Cartridges". Given the vast amount of bad information that has been floating around for years regarding the correct way to chamber for an Ackley Improved cartridge, this book is a breath of fresh air. Over the years I have attended the NRA summer gunsmithing classes at several schools. For twenty consecutive summers I spent 2 to 4 weeks at the schools that offered the courses and instructors that I was most interested in learning from, all renowned in their fields. Some were very knowledgeable, some were at least competent in their fields, some were good at instructing, and some clearly wished they were somewhere else. I was taught at least 4 different "One True Way" to chamber Ackley's cartridges, and none were what Ackley taught in his books. Some worked OK, and some demonstrably did not.

Fred makes the whole process so stunningly simple and understandable that any competent machinist/gunsmith can turn out perfect Ackley chambers that allow the standard cartridge to be used and the resulting Ackley case to look just like P. O. designed it. Fred is highly competent and respected as a gunsmith, wildcatter, cartridge designer, and machinist. He has had a vast amount of experience and training from some of the best gunsmiths in the business. He has run businesses for other people as well as his own, and is definitely well versed in the material he presents. All of that would be impressive in its own right, but the most important thing he brings to this enterprise is clarity of vision and the ability to bring that clarity to a student. From my own experience, I can attest this is a rare combination.

I have known Fred for a number of years from his books, and have had the pleasure of having published his articles on different aspects of reloading and gunsmithing for our company's "GunTech" magazine. He is an entertaining, informative, and thoroughly professional writer. He has also instructed videos on designing, chambering, and loading wildcat cartridges. He even showed how to make your own chamber reamers in such a simple way that the average gunsmith machinist can easily manage the task. He has my great admiration for making the seemingly arcane understandable, and I am looking forward to the rest of the books in this series.

Jack Landis

Editor, GunTech Magazine &
Technical Services Manager,
American Gunsmithing Institute

Preface

This booklet is the first of many planned works that provide instruction in the correct and safe methods of gunsmithing.

Specifically, this treatise discusses Ackley Improved cartridges. We will not teach you how to install and chamber a barrel here, we handle that information in, "Chambering Rifle Barrels for Accuracy". In this book we will in detail help you to understand the special details related to chambering for Ackley Improved designs.

There are many books about gunsmithing; those that contain any great amount of technical information are long outdated. Still more of them are written by writers who have never made a living gunsmithing. All such books provide interesting information and some methods remain unchanged. However, as tools and technology change so does the process of gunsmithing.

In many gunsmithing books subjects are spoken of in such a general way that the novice has a difficult time deciphering just what is intended. When you're learning a complicated process a clear understanding of the basics is equally as important as learning the nuances of advanced concepts. This booklet and those that will follow in the "Gunsmithing Student Handbook Series" are designed to be of value to gunsmiths at all skill levels.

It's important to realize that there is more than one method of gunsmithing a problem that will produce quality results. So, no claim is made that I am covering all the possibilities. Only that the methods taught are tried and true. You can and should seek other methods and ideas to achieve the best quality work you can produce. I hope this series of books will become an important part of your tool kit as well.

Fred Zeglin
Kalispell, MT
2014

Acknowledgements

Special Thanks to Sporting Arms and Ammunition Manufacturers' Institute, Inc. (SAAMI) for the use of their prints in this booklet. http://www.saami.org

Of course thanks go to P.O. Ackley. After all, this booklet is a direct result of the design work of P.O. Ackley. His improved designs have afforded shooters with many happy hours of entertainment on the range and in the field.

Dave Kiff of Pacific Tool & Gauge for reamer prints and accurate information.

Table of Contents

Defining Ackley Improved Cartridges

"The only wildcats worth considering are those that will accept factory ammunition in the same chamber, as exemplified by the Ackley Improved .257 Roberts..."[1] Fred Ness.

P.O. Ackley is the undisputed King of Improved cartridges and maybe of wildcats in general. He was active in gunsmithing from 1936 until his passing in 1989. Ackley was probably not the originator of fireformed "improved" cartridge designs, but he was definitely the guy who popularized it, and more importantly P.O. Ackley standardized the improved cartridge concept. What I mean by that is that he created a simple understandable headspace method for these designs.

Before we go too far, lets define an "Improved" cartridge. According to Ackley, "An improved cartridge is a factory cartridge that has been fired in an improved chamber and thus has its form changed. In other words, a rifle made to handle an improved cartridge for example the Improved 257 (Roberts), will still handle factory ammunition, but the fireformed cases can be reloaded, or handloaded, to considerably higher velocities without danger to the shooter."[2]

Ackley defining a wildcat, "A wildcat cartridge cannot be obtained commercially or will not handle factory ammunition of any form."[3] In short wildcat brass must be formed in dies before it will ever fit the gun it was intended for. It should be noted that when Ackley talks about commercial brass here he is referring to mass produced factory ammunition, not boutique ammo makers.

After some trial and error Ackley came to a conclusion as to what degree of body taper was necessary for reliable extraction, and what shoulder angles worked best. Ackley was of the opinion

---

[1] Practical Dope on the Big Bores, by Fred C. Ness, 1948
[2] Measuring Heaspace, by P.O. Ackley, Shooting Times, June, 1960
[3] Measuring Heaspace, by P.O. Ackley, Shooting Times, June, 1960

personally that a shoulder angle of 28 degrees was optimum for efficiency, accuracy, reliable headspacing, and easy case forming.

"Most of our 22 cases, such as the 228 Ackley, the Improved Zippers, the 17 caliber, are all 28 degree shoulder. We can see very little difference in small changes of shoulder angle. We have tried the 45 degree shoulders but did not like the results; we can see no increase in efficiency over the 30 degree or even the 28 degree but with the too-sharp angles the head space is hard to maintain."[4] Wrote P.O. Ackley to Charles Landis.

Standard Headspace Gauges

Even though Ackley preferred the 28 degree shoulder, his clients wanted the sharper 40 degree shoulder, and at 40 degrees his tools lasted longer than with sharper angles. He knew from experience that this would not harm accuracy to any important degree, and that it had no real effect on ballistics. It was simply a marketing issue, clients perceived that a sharper shoulder was somehow better. Customers want what they want, so give it to them, especially if there is no significant difference.

---

[4] Twenty-Two Caliber Varmint Rifles by Charles S. Landis, 1946

Understanding Headspace…

Before we discuss chambering it is important to understand how headspace is measured for all standard cartridge case designs. Ackley explained basic headspace methods in his "Handbook for Shooters and Reloaders". Nothing has really changed in the field since that time, however this author will reiterate the information here and perhaps with different wording it will help more shooters, reloaders, and gunsmiths to fully grasp what is happening when headspace is in question.

1. Rimless, semi-rimmed and rebated cases utilize the Datum Line to establish headspace. This method of measurement refers to a specified point on the shoulder of the cartridge that is a predetermined diameter. Headspace is measured from the bolt face to the datum line. By way of example the 270 Winchester's datum line is the point along the shoulder of the chamber or gauge that measures .375" in diameter. Depending on the specific case the datum line varies with the size of the case. Cases that are registered with SAAMI will have dimensions specified on drawings for that case and approved by SAAMI. Wildcats can and should have a datum line too.

    In the drawing on the next page the measurement along the shoulder diameter called out as .375 is the datum line. Headspace specific dimensions are marked with this symbol: ⊗

2. Rimmed cases are headspaced by the thickness of the rim, The distance from the bolt face to the front edge of the cartridge rim is the headspace. The forward edge of the case rim should fully contact the back of the barrel when the bolt is in the closed/locked position. Rim thicknesses vary, with the majority of modern cartridges ranging from .060" to .070".

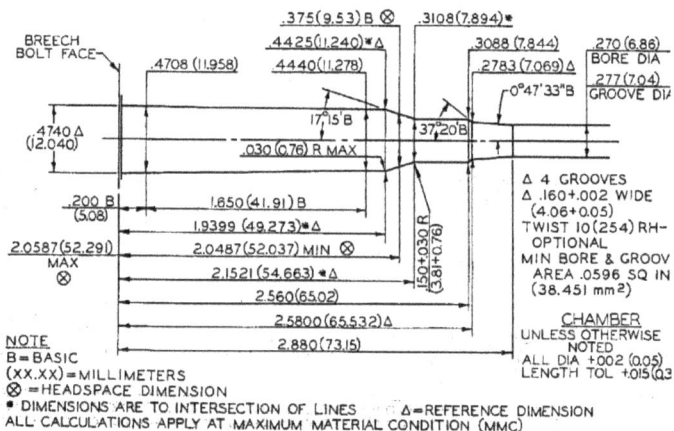

BREECH BOLT FACE	.375(9.53) B ⊗ .3108(7.894)• .4425(11.240)•Δ .4708 (11.958) .4440(11.278) .3088 (7.844) 270 (6.86) BORE DIA .2783 (7.069) Δ .277(7.04) GROOVE DIA

.4740 Δ (12.040)

17°15' B   37°20' B

.030 (0.76) R MAX

0°47'33" B

.200 B (5.08)

1.650 (41.91) B

1.9399 (49.273)•Δ

2.0587 (52.291) MAX ⊗

2.0487 (52.037) MIN ⊗

2.1521 (54.663) •Δ

2.560 (65.02)

2.5800 (65.532) Δ

2.880 (73.15)

.150+.030 R (3.81+0.76)

Δ 4 GROOVES
Δ .160+.002 WIDE
(4.06+0.05)
TWIST 10(254) RH-
OPTIONAL
MIN BORE & GROOV
AREA .0596 SQ IN
(38.451 mm2)

CHAMBER
UNLESS OTHERWISE NOTED
ALL DIA +.002 (0.05)
LENGTH TOL +.015 (0.3

NOTE
B = BASIC
(XX.XX) = MILLIMETERS
⊗ = HEADSPACE DIMENSION
• DIMENSIONS ARE TO INTERSECTION OF LINES   Δ = REFERENCE DIMENSION
ALL CALCULATIONS APPLY AT MAXIMUM MATERIAL CONDITION (MMC)

5

*Note that in the print below for the 30-30 Winchester there is a datum point at .375 along the shoulder but it is **not** called out as a headspace measurement.*

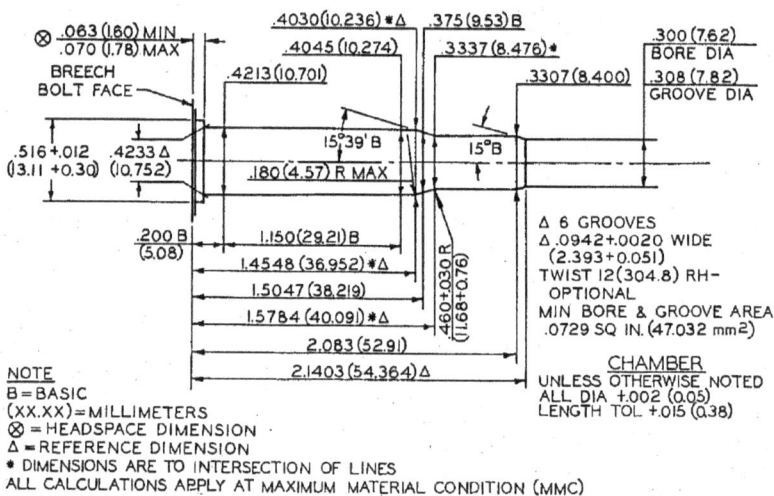

⊗ .063 (1.60) MIN   .070 (1.78) MAX

.4030 (10.236) •Δ   .375 (9.53) B
.4045 (10.274)   .3337 (8.476)•

.300 (7.62) BORE DIA

BREECH BOLT FACE

.4213 (10.701)

.3307 (8.400)   .308 (7.82) GROOVE DIA

.516 +.012 (13.11 +0.30)   .4233 Δ (10.752)

15°39' B

15° B

.180 (4.57) R MAX

.200 B (5.08)

1.150 (29.21) B

1.4548 (36.952) •Δ

1.5047 (38.219)

1.5784 (40.09) •Δ

2.083 (52.91)

2.1403 (54.364) Δ

.460+.030 R (11.68+0.76)

Δ 6 GROOVES
Δ .0942+.0020 WIDE
(2.393+0.051)
TWIST 12(304.8) RH-
OPTIONAL
MIN BORE & GROOVE AREA
.0729 SQ IN. (47.032 mm2)

CHAMBER
UNLESS OTHERWISE NOTED
ALL DIA +.002 (0.05)
LENGTH TOL +.015 (0.38)

NOTE
B = BASIC
(XX.XX) = MILLIMETERS
⊗ = HEADSPACE DIMENSION
Δ = REFERENCE DIMENSION
• DIMENSIONS ARE TO INTERSECTION OF LINES
ALL CALCULATIONS APPLY AT MAXIMUM MATERIAL CONDITION (MMC)

6

3. Belted cases measure headspace from the face of a fully locked bolt to the front edge of the belt. For standard magnums based on the H&H case design this measurement

---

[5] 270 Winchester chamber print, SAAMI.org
[6] 30-30 Winchester, SAAMI.org

is .220". At the time of this writing the only exceptions to this measurement are the 240 Weatherby which is a belted 30-06 case, according to SAAMI it headspaces at .219", and the other exception is the .378 or .460 Weatherby case head, this family of cases headspace at .252".

*The print below represents belted magnum cases, as with the rimmed cases mentioned on the previous page, even though there is a datum point called out on the shoulder it is **not** a headspace measurement.*

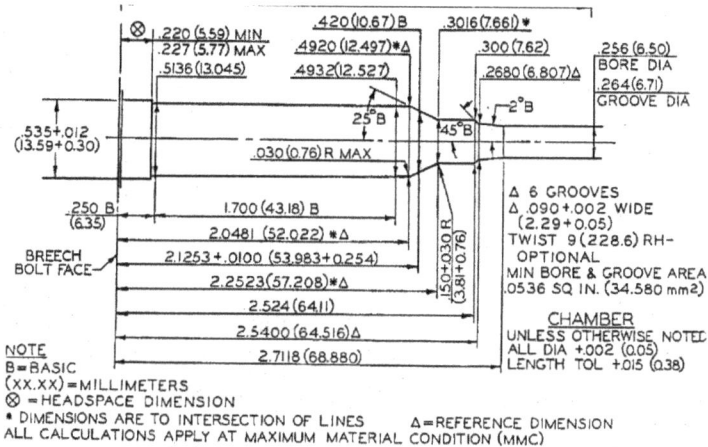

It is vitally important that the gunsmith understand correct headspace methods for the various systems in use today. This knowledge can save you many hours of head scratching when diagnosing problems in firearms.

Unfortunately over the years many wildcatters have failed to establish headspace standards for their creations. As a result when you pick up a used wildcat or improved rifle, it is often necessary to chamber cast the rifle if no dies or fired cases come with it.

Often gun bugs will gripe that they wish Ackley had produced drawings and set standards. In truth of fact, he did, in his 1959 edition of "Handbook for Shooters & Reloaders" and in his later

---

[7] 264 Winchester Magnum, SAAMI.org

"Pocket Manual" he published not only his most popular cartridge dimensions but many other wildcats as well. So the truth is that many gun bugs need to do more research, the information is often available in print somewhere.

Unfortunately some of the problems we run into with wildcats today come from reamer makers not having the original information either. They walk a fine line between serving the desires of clients and educating them as to what is already out there.

Today the reamer makers have developed an understanding that if "Joe Gunsmith" sends in a design and says he wants to hold it as a proprietary design, it's good business to honor that request.

Pros and Cons of Proprietary Cartridges

On the whole it's more profitable to allow full public access to the correct information. I simply ask the reamer makers to never release a reamer with my wildcat cartridge name if their customer changes any dimensions. I just ask that they give it a new name if there is any modification to the dimensions. This protects me when I sell dies, brass, or ammo.

SAAMI will accept drawings of wildcats for their archives, they will not register the design as they would with a SAAMI approved design, but at least the "official" dimensions are permanently recorded.

The firearms industry is changing rapidly, today we can have short run custom brass or ammo made for any wildcat with proper headstamps, something that was totally cost prohibitive in the past. It's still not cheap, and it takes time, but at least you can have properly headstamped brass without spending tens of thousands of dollars. So, its more important than ever to "standardize" improved and wildcat designs.

The liability associated with building rifles with non-standard headspace is growing with our society's penchant for lawsuits. When I say Non-standard headspace I mean, "outside of industry standard practices". The shooting public is often lazy about educating themselves. As a gunsmith you must protect yourself from liability by educating yourself, and then passing that education along to clients.

Ackley discusses this problem in his handbooks, saying that, "the gunsmith will find it necessary to determine the headspace himself as nearly as possible. This means there will be considerable variation in the headspace of some wildcat cartridges as they are chambered for by different gunsmiths."[8] This is no longer the case, you can order gauges from the reamer maker with the chamber reamer, so there is no reason for variations in headspace measurement.

Back in Ackley's day his cure for headspace problems was to supply dies with the rifle when he delivered it, a solution that worked for him. This would be an easy way for you to protect yourself and to make a little more money on the job, by supplying dies.

According to P. O. Ackley, "Shoulder angles in chambers and also on factory cartridges vary more than one would think. Sometimes the shoulder angle of the chamber is a little bit steeper' than that found on the factory cartridges. Then, when the neck is enlarged, the point of contact is changed, resulting in excessive head-space. If the angle in the chamber is the same as the angle on the new cartridge, the headspace will not have to be changed." Ackley is pointing out the need to carefully check headspace.

Headspace adjustment, if needed, may necessitate setting the barrel back a turn.[9] It is and should be standard practice to set back a barrel when it is rechambering for an improved rimless or rebated

---

[8] Handbook for Shooters and Reloaders, Vol. 1, by P.O. Ackley, 1962

[9] Gun Digest, "New Zing for Old Barrels" Dan Cotterman, 1967

case. **This is not a suggestion;** it is an axiom in gunsmithing, if you plan to build safe and reliable firearms. The relationship between the brass and chamber requires setting back a barrel when it is rechambered for an improved rimless or rebated case. In other words, the primary reason for setting the barrel back is to insure correct headspace so that factory ammo can **safely** be fired in the "Improved" chamber.

Ackley is referring to tolerances in the quotes above. Many shooters and even self proclaimed gunsmiths are not aware of tolerances. When manufacturing large quantities of anything including guns and ammo, it is necessary to allow for variations in the product as tools wear and materials vary.

Novice shooters often think of factory ammunition as perfect, <u>it is not</u>, if all is as it should be the ammunition you find in your local store falls within the allowed tolerances as provided by the Sporting Arms and Ammunition Manufactures Institute (SAAMI), the governing body for firearms dimension and standards in the United States.

SAAMI is an accredited standards developer for the American National Standards Institute (ANSI). As an accredited standards developer, SAAMI sets standards for industry test methods, definitive proof loads, and ammunition performance specifications which are subject to ANSI review and various ANSI criteria. In other words, there are clearly defined values by which firearms and ammunition are produced within specified limits.

As a wildcatter one need not fly by the seat of your pants, you can apply the same tolerances to your designs as are used by SAAMI and know that you're working within reasonable limits.

P.O. Ackley discussing Ackley Improved case designs for rimless bottleneck cases said, "When checking the headspace, a standard "Go" gauge with .004" ground off the head is the proper one to use. In other words, the headspace has to be minimum-minus .004" in order to prevent case head separations." *The standard*

"Go" gauge for the caliber becomes the "No-Go" gauge for the Ackley Improved chamber. Of course, this is in reference to rimless or rebated cases only.

As a result most shops will buy an Ackley go gauge and simply use the gauges they already have for the parent case to provide the no-go. If you adopt this method it's a good practice to use gauges from the same maker to avoid tolerance stacking issues.

It is possible to order gauges that are marked specifically as Ackley go and no-go. While buying these extra gauges adds tooling costs, such gauges do reduce confusion if you find all this just too much to keep straight.

Brass, Reloading, and Headspace…

Ackley commented on forming brass and possible problems if the headspace is not correct; "When fire forming new cases, separation troubles may not appear the first time a case is fired but there is a weakness created the first time a case is fired, unless the headspace is sufficiently tight to create a crush fit on the unformed new case."[10]

In a letter to another gunsmith Ackley wrote, "When a factory cartridge is chambered in the Improved chamber, it should require some force to close the bolt. When the empty case is extracted you can see a definite ring right at the base of the shoulder where it contacted the chamber."[11]

At right: You can see where the factory case made contact with the improved chamber.

---

[10] Guns & Ammo, Q&A, P.O. Ackley, February 1967
[11] Letter to Bevan King, October 23, 1974

Most reloaders I talk to and a fair number of gunsmiths as well, do not realize that reloading dies can be used to set or adjust headspace on the brass. Most of the dies I have checked have .005" of crush available to the reloader. This means that you could easily move the shoulder of a factory case to below minimum length (that is the definition of excessive headspace in brass or ammo).

Ackley reported that in his day some dies were as much as .020" short which would really cause problems for an unwitting reloader. Likewise, dies that do not allow any crush at the shoulder can be a problem.

The idea is for the end user to adjust the dies to make the best possible match to their chamber.

The proper way to set dies is to run them down to touch the shell holder, then back off a half turn and test them. Brass should be sized the length of the neck and just kiss the shoulder. The only time you need to "bump the shoulder" is when the brass has grown too long and is making the bolt hard to close. You will normally see this after your brass has been reloaded more than once.

Three to four loadings, according to most sources, is about the point where you will have no choice but to bump the shoulder back. This is easily checked by placing resized cases in the chamber of your gun, close the bolt, if there is unusual resistance then the case has grown longer and need the shoulder bumped.

Writers talk about the need to check your brass in the chamber of your gun when reloading, they are aware that you can have trouble closing the bolt. I am not sure they all understand that you can go too far and cause headspace issues by making the case too short at the shoulder (excessive headspace in the ammo).

Nine times out of ten when a client claims that the gunsmith built his gun with excessive headspace the problem is with the reloader not the gunsmith. Ackley out and out said that many of the guys who get into wildcats have little or no understanding of headspace and therefore should not own a wildcat. I am inclined to agree, if you're too lazy to learn about the tools and how they are intended to function then you're a danger to yourself the poor guy at the next shooting bench.

If you're a gunsmith then you need to take it upon yourself to instruct the client in the proper use of reloading dies. Especially when they have confessed that this is their first wildcat or improved cartridge. In so doing you will head off those clients who complain that you built it wrong by making them aware of the proper use of reloading tools in conjunction with their new gun.

If the bolt is hard to open on the first reload fired you're probably loading too hot, back off the powder charge. Alternatively, check the length of the throat in the chamber vs. the way the bullet is seated. If the bullet is touching or jammed into the lands, pressures can jump 6000 to 8000 PSI, a significant amount.
There are several products available to the reloader and gunsmith that allow the measurement of cases for headspace.

Forster offers the Datum Dial™, RCBS has the Precision Mic™, Redding's Instant Indicator™ headspace and bullet comparator, Sinclair Bump Gage, Wilson and Lyman both offer case gauges that check headspace and length of the brass and Hornady offers the Lock-n-Load™ headspace tool set are all examples of tools made specifically to help the reloader address headspace in their reloads. So there are numerous ways the gunsmith and reloader alike can keep track of headspace in cartridges and chamberings.

For the gunsmith a tool that can be used on nearly any cartridge would be the best choice simply because of the ability the check any project you might be dealing with. By checking your clients reloads against fired cases from the gun you can determine if the client is creating headspace problems. Then definitively show them the problem. Education is key.

Chambering an Improved Rimmed Case...

To be clear this book is not intended to teach you how to chamber a barrel. It is only intended to discuss the specifics of working with Ackley cartridge designs and how to headspace such cartridges. The writer assumes you know how to ream a chamber.

Rimmed cases are the easiest of all Improved or wildcat cases to chamber for. The rim is the headspace control feature on these cases. The rim is trapped between the bolt face and the back of the barrel. So if the rim is headspaced correctly you can have almost any shape of case fire-formed beyond the rim, so long as it will extract. The receiver of the firearm is not sentient; it does not care what the chamber looks like. So rimmed cases utilize standard headspace gauges for the parent cartridge, no Ackley gauges are needed.

A side note: Rimmed headspace gauges do not normally have the full shape of the chamber, they are normally just a plug gauge with the rim being the measuring tool. The plug simply makes it easier to handle the rim gauge.

At right: A rimmed headspace gauge.
As mentioned above, this gauge does not look anything like the chamber it is designed to headspace. Only the rims diameter and thickness matter.

There is no need to set the barrel back on a rimmed cartridge when you convert it to an Improved design! Why? Because the rim controls headspace, the fact that the shoulder will be moved forward and the neck shortened has exactly **_NO effect_** on headspace.

Reamers for improved cases normally have the rim cutter integral to their design. Simply paint the rim cut in the barrel with machinist's blue, when the rim cutter gets close to this material just watch close, as soon as it scratches the machinists blue, stop reaming. Utilizing this method there is no danger of changing the headspace of the gun in the process of 'Improving' the chamber.

'Improved' cases of the rimmed variety often incorporate a shorter neck, thus the shoulder is moved forward, this is combined with increased shoulder diameter to achieve greater case capacity. Often rimmed cases benefit the most from an 'Improved' design, simply because they gain a much higher percentage of case capacity.

Another advantage the sharper shoulder of the improved case design is that cases will stretch less. This is simply because it is hard for the brass to make two sharp turns at the shoulder, as apposed to the long tapered design of many factory rimmed cases.

Chambering an Improved Belted Chamber...

What was said of rimmed cases is also true of belted cases.

Belted designs headspace on the belt much the same way rimmed cases headspace on the rim. The distance between the bolt face and the belt cut in the barrel is the headspace for these cartridges. Like the rimmed designs, 'Improved' belted cases use the standard headspace gauges for the parent case, no Ackley gauges.

While it is possible to use machinists blue as suggested with the rimmed case, you will quickly find that it is much harder to determine if the machinist blue has been scratched, there is simply much less area to view. Consequently, it is a good idea to set the barrel back when reaming for a belted magnum improved case. If the barrel is slick with no sight holes drilled in it, and no extractor cut, you can set it back a few thousandths of an inch so that that bolt will not close on the go gauge. Then rechamber with the improved reamer until the go gauge will allow the bolt to close normally.

If your barrel has sight holes or an extractor cut it will be need to be set back a full turn to align or "time" the barrel with the receiver properly, otherwise your sights will not be at top dead center. Once the barrel is set back you can simply rechamber to correct headspace.

Chambering Rimless or Rebated Improved Chambers...

Ackley Improved cartridges in this category seem to receive the most abuse at the hands of hobbyists and local gunsmiths who do not understand the proper headspace of Ackley Improved designs.

At Right: Rimless Headspace Gauge measures headspace from the bolt face to the angled shoulder.

P.O. Ackley did establish specific headspace dimensions for all his Improved case designs. The process is extremely simple and for this reason alone folks seem to think they need to make it more complex. Keep it simple.

The most important innovation that Ackley brought to the "improved" concept was with regard to bottleneck rimless cases. He chose the simplest of mechanical solutions to insure that his improved cases would safely fire factory loads. He shortened the chamber by .004" (4/1000 of an inch). Because the factory case is then a crush fit between the bolt face and the junction of the neck and shoulder, proper headspace is insured.

To clarify: Headspace gauges for Ackley Improved cartridges in rimless, semi-rimless or rebated cases utilize a Go gauge that is .004" shorter than the standard for caliber Go gauge (standard:

referring to the parent cartridge) and retain the original shoulder angle for the parent chamber on the gauge.

The standard for caliber Go gauge becomes the No-Go gauge for the Ackley chamber. You will note that if you follow these simple guidelines there is no confusion about the headspace measurements for "Ackley Improved" designs in rimless or rebated cases.

Folks seem to get confused between the set up for a rimless bottleneck case and a rimmed or belted case when discussing 'Improved" chamberings.

Rimless and rebated cases are the case designs which <u>always</u> require a barrel set back to be properly headspaced. Headspace on an Ackley Improved rimless or rebated designs is shorter than standard. The shorter headspace means you have *no choice* but to set the barrel back if you want correct headspace.

*NOTE: When we discuss the length of the headspace gauge we are talking about the **length from the bolt face to the datum line on the shoulder**. The actual length of the gauge is of NO-CONCERN. The datum line is a point along the shoulder where the gauge measures a specified diameter (see SAAMI or chamber reamer prints for specifics). This paragraph may seem silly to some, but I answer this question at least once a week.*

Why does the shorter gauge work?

A traditional Ackley Go gauge has the <u>same</u> shoulder angle as the parent case but they are shorter. This ingenious method effectively controls headspace with factory cartridges in the new larger, 'Improved' chamber. The parent (factory cartridge) Go-gauge becomes the No-go for the new chamber. This system works because the parent Go-gauge is .004" longer than the Ackley gauge, this is exactly the same measurement as between any standard Go-gauge and No-go gauge set.

Example: 30-06 Ackley Improved go-gauge is used with the standard 30-06 go-gauge as the no-go gauge.

The only place the factory case will touch in the new chamber, that matters, is the bolt face and the junction of the neck and shoulder on the case. It will actually slightly crush the case shoulder when you close the bolt on the factory round. If you eject such a case unfired you will normally see a shinny area on the shoulder where the case was crushed just a little (pictured on page 18). This crush fit maintains proper headspace during the fire-forming process.

Below: Note the factory cartridge on bottom touches the Ackley chamber at the junction of the neck and shoulder as explained above. Top a fully formed case in the same chambering.

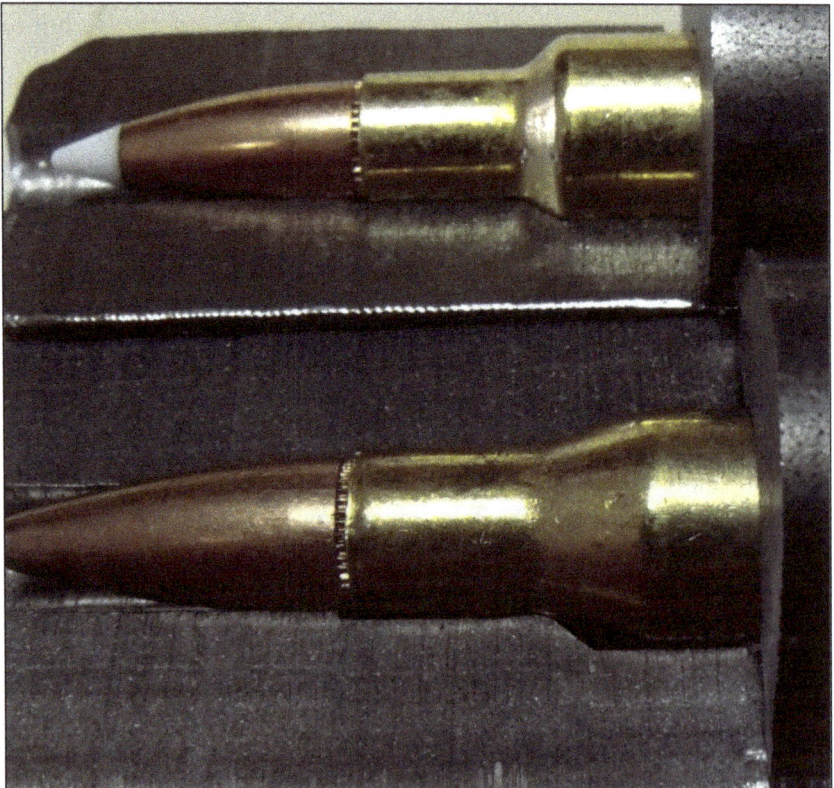

Ackley wrote this comment to another gunsmith concerning polishing chambers, "For improved cartridges where fire forming will be done by using factory ammunition, you have to be extremely careful not to round the corner at the junction of the neck and the shoulder, because this will increase the headspace dangerously on factory ammunition."[12]

In recent years, several of the commercial reamer makers have decided to offer Ackley gauges with the "Improved" shoulder angle. This change represents one more way that novices can be confused about the headspace on Ackley Improved cases. However, all such gauges this author has seen still provide the same headspace measurements, so the finished product is the same as Ackley intended, only the math is different.

P.O. Ackley created a simple and reliable method to headspace his "Improved" designs. It's not an earth shattering principal, but if followed it makes the gunsmith's and the reloader's job easy. Ackley's understanding that a uniform and simple system would be beneficial provides a glimpse into his intelligence.

---

[12]   Letter to Bevan King, May 25, 1973

Shoulder angle of the top gauge is standard for the parent case. The bottom gauge has the Improved 40 degree shoulder.

Even though these two gauges look very different, they still produce chambers of the same length. It's a simple geometry problem.

Fire Forming Cases

Rimless and Rebated cases are easy to fire form in Ackley chambers if the headspace is correctly set as described earlier.

Simply fire factory ammunition of the parent caliber in the chamber to form the Improved case. The result will be a velocity slightly reduced as compared to firing the same load in a standard chamber. This loss of velocity is primarily as a result of energy being used to form the brass, secondarily because the larger volume of the improved chamber requires more powder to produce the same velocity.

Rimmed or belted designs headspace on the rim or belt respectively. So you can fire factory ammo and in most instances it will produce good results, even though the shoulder is often blown forward on these designs. One exception would be using old previously fired brass, often it is too brittle and will split during fire forming. So using new unfired cases is recommended for fire forming. Or if you anneal older brass it will form with greater success.

If you happen to have a wildcat that has a large amount of forming to do, firing factory ammo will sometimes cause an unacceptable loss of brass to split cases. This happens because the cases expands so quickly that if there is a flaw or weak spot in the brass it will pop like an over filled balloon. One example of this would be the 219 Zipper Ackley Improved. If you experience this there are two possible solutions:

1. Try annealing the neck and shoulder down the body as much as half way. Make sure you do not anneal the case head or the thick web area just above the head. Annealing the head will greatly reduce the cases ability to handle pressure. Once annealed, load the cases as normal and try fire forming a few. Initially, don't load more cases than

you are willing to pull bullets from, just in case the results are poor.

2. Fire form using corn meal or "Cream of Wheat". George Nonte in his book, "Home Guide to Cartridge Conversions"[13] tells how to develop fire forming loads using **no bullet**. Ken Howell in his book, "Custom Cartridges"[14] expanded on the concept.

First insert a spent primer (for safety) in an unformed case. Fill the case with Bullseye® pistol powder to the top of the neck **(DO NOT FIRE!)**. Then pour this charge into the pan of your powder scale and weigh the charge. Divide that amount by 10, so that 1/10 of the total volume will become your starting load.

Now take that 10% load whatever it is for your case and put it in your normally primed case. Tear a single sheet of toilet paper in quarters, insert one quarter as a wad over the powder charge. Now fill the rest of the case with your inert filler (corn meal, or fine ground hot cereal, etc., dry of course). You will want to place a wad of some sort over the cereal so it does not spill. Bees wax, bullet lube, or toilet paper work, the over wad must be light enough so that it can be blown down the barrel without doing any damage.

You are ready to fire form a case. **Keep in mind even without a bullet these loads could be deadly, use all normal gun safety practices.**

---

13   The Home Guide to Cartridge Conversions, George C. Nonte Jr., 1961
14   Custom Cartridges, Ken Howell, 1995

Pointing in a safe direction fire the first load, if the case is not fully formed bump your 10% load by ½ grain at a time until you get a fully formed case. It may take some testing to get a load that fully forms the case.

It is possible to generate dangerous pressures if you use too much powder even with an inert filler load, so be careful. The interesting thing about this method is that it will often form cases without any loss to ruptures or split necks when a factory load will cause ruptures.

L.R. Wallack wrote this method up for American Rifleman's "Dope Bag", after describing the method he said, "I then did 10 cases with this load with no splits and all formed nicely. Such success has been practically unheard of, as anyone who has formed cases for this wildcat well knows. I have no hesitation, therefore, in recommending the method."[15]

---

[15]   American Rifleman, Dope Bag, L.R. Wallack, July, 1956

Selection of Appropriate Actions.

Feeding of wildcats in Mauser 98 actions is often misunderstood or overlooked by gunsmiths and hobbyists. If you look at the magazine box of a 98 Mauser you will notice that in most examples there is a recoil shoulder machined into the box. This shoulder is placed in the box at a point where the original factory cartridge's shoulder would have been in the magazine. It's purpose is to prevent the cases from moving forward under recoil, a great design feature that protects projectiles from damage and prevents them from being forced into the cartridge under recoil.

When a new cartridge is fit to a 98 Mauser it is a good idea to see where the shoulder of the new case mates up with the recoil shoulder in the magazine box and or feed rails in the action. If the cartridge shoulder is ahead of the recoil shoulder in the magazine it can cause the alignment of the cases in the box to interfere with smooth feeding.

A bigger issue with feeding in a 98 can be the way the rails of the action are cut. Often they are setup for a specific length cartridge. If the shoulder of your case is too far forward and the case is pushed toward the center of the magazine too much it is possible for a cartridge to jump out of the magazine early, eliminating the advantage of controlled round feeding.

Your gunsmith should modify the magazine and occasionally the rails of the action so that case stays in the magazine until the correct time insuring the controlled round feed continues to work. This is simply a matter of cutting the recoil shoulder further forward. On rare occasions you may find an action that is too narrow in the feed ramp area, some careful filing or grinding will fix this problem. The feed rails must be polished after modifications or the brass will be badly scratched or dented in feeding, or it may not feed at all.

Nearly any commercially made actions made since World War II will handle these cartridges. Generally speaking if the action is available in the factory version (i.e. 30-06) of the Ackley cartridge (30-06 AI) then it will be capable of handling the Improved version of the cartridge without any change to the magazine.

The most common error in selecting actions are selecting an action with the wrong bolt face diameter; make sure your action can be adapted for the correct size bolt face.

The next most common error is selecting an action that is not well suited to the cartridge in question, magazine too short or too long. Choosing a rimmed cartridge and trying to force it into a rimless action would be another example of a poor choice.

Rimmed Cartridges have very limited use in bolt action rifles. The British SMLE, the P-14 Enfield, Mosin Nagant and Siamese Mauser are examples of bolt guns that use rimmed cases.

Rimmed cases are well suited to single shots, double rifles and lever actions as a rule. In today's market and considering popular firearms, single shots and levers will be the best choices for rimmed cases going forward in terms of availability and cost.

From the chart on the next page it should be obvious that cartridges with an increase in capacity greater than three percent are the ones worth working with. Ackley would have been the first to tell you this.

It seems silly to write this, but I have heard this comment too often to ignore it; To attain the increased velocity in the Ackley Improved case you will have to burn more powder than you did in the parent cartridge. The statement is usually framed as a negative, it shows a lack of understanding as to why Ackley Improved designs are desirable.

Comparing Ackley Chambers to Factory

Factory Cartridge	Bullet Weight In Grains	Factory Velocity	Ackley Improved Velocity	% Increase of Velocity
219 Zipper	55	3110	3450	10.9
22-250 Remington	50	3719	3947	6.1
6mm Remington	75	3400	3553	4.5
243 Winchester	100	2960	3089	4.4
25-35 WCF	117	2230	2579	15.7
250 Savage	100	2820	3129	11
257 Roberts	117	2780	3120	12.2
25-06 *	117	2990	3051	2
6.5-06 A-Square	140	2954	3095	4.8
270 Winchester *	150	3010	3048	1.3
7mm-08	150	2823	2865	1.5
7x57 Mauser	160	2690	2791	3.7
280 Remington	160	2795	2988	6.7
30-30 WCF	150	2370	2535	6.8
30-40 Krag	180	2445	2740	12.1
30-06 Springfield	150	2900	3117	7.3
30-06 Springfield	180	2690	2865	6.7
300 H&H	220	2565	2835	10.5
348 Winchester	250	2297	2470	7.7
35 Whelen	250	2400	2575	7.4
375 H&H	250	2690	2940	9.2
375 H&H	300	2600	2800	7.7

*P.O. did not recommend these cartridges in the improved form.

Improved cases need more powder, it's as if you have bored and stroked an engine, it will then burn more fuel to produce more horse power. An Ackley Improved chamber is the same, it will burn more fuel and deliver more velocity.

If you do not add the fuel then there was no reason to increase the size of the chamber. Factory loaded parent cases will produce less velocity in an Ackley chamber, because they are fire forming the brass and the chamber is larger in volume than the factory parent chamber would be.

Frequently people state that Ackley was reckless or ran excessive pressures without regard for the dangers. That is totally incorrect. Ackley was well aware of the limits of various guns and how pressure affects the firearm.

Ackley utilized chronographs and pressure test equipment during his career. Today we have relatively inexpensive tools for testing pressure like the Pressure Trace™, so there is no reason to run excessive pressures and we can easily demonstrate the value of Ackley Improved designs.

280 Ackley Improved Controversy…

There was a fair amount of buzz among Ackley fans when Nosler decided to take the 280 Ackley Improved to SAAMI in 2006. Nosler wanted to pay Ackley the honor of using his name, they even called the Ackley family and asked permission to use the name as a courtesy, both are admirable acts.

While it's not all that unusual for a company to legitimize a wildcat, it is with few exceptions unusual for the cartridge to retain the designer's original name. There are reasons for this, whenever a factory decides to bring a wildcat to commercial production they are concerned about the fact that many gunsmiths have copied a wildcat but are <u>not</u> diligent about headspacing it as designed. Or large numbers or older guns chambered for the cartridge questionable strength.

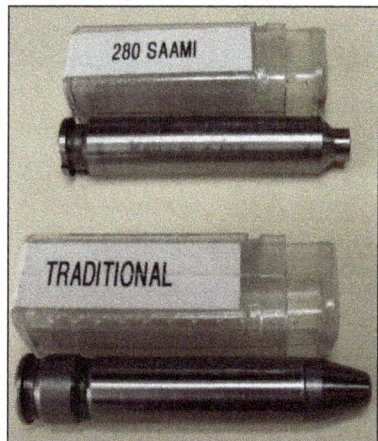

When Nosler contemplated bringing a fifty-something year old wildcat to the industry as a factory offering they, looked around the see how the cartridge had been treated during its history. Many gunsmiths are vague on the proper headspace for an Ackley Improved bottle-neck cartridge; which is why I am writing this book.

As explained in detail earlier in this book, all you do is use the Ackley go gauge in conjunction with the standard go gauge for caliber as the no-go. i.e. Use a 280 AI go gauge with a 280 Remington go gauge as the no-go.

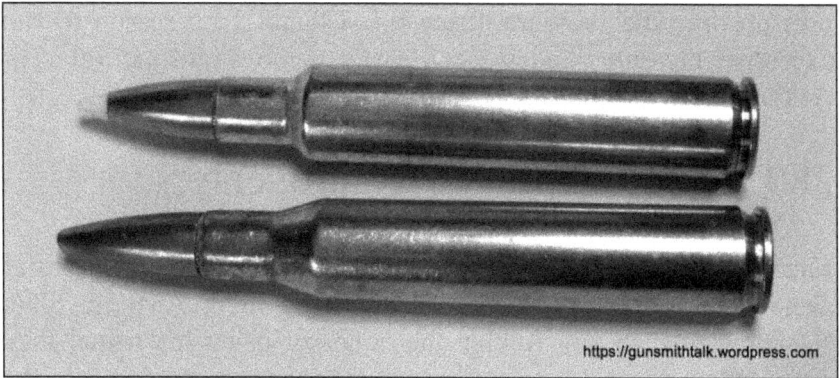

280 Ackley Improved, Nosler brass on top and 280 Remington on bottom.

Ackley knew what he was doing, here's the proof, the difference in length between the two gauges just mentioned is .004" (4/1000 of an inch). The difference between a standard 280 Remington go gauge and no-go gage is .004". So when you chamber a factory 280 case in a 280 AI chamber it is crushed at the point where the neck and the shoulder meet. This crush holds the case tight against the bolt face for safe fire forming (same as with all rimless bottleneck cases).

All sounds pretty simple, right? Well, apparently not.

Many gunsmiths in the trade fail to follow this simple formula. So, their "Ackley" chambers may be too long or too short depending on how they misapply the headspace gauges. To complicate matters further, Nosler supposedly found out that Remington's custom shop had been setting the headspace on their

280 Ackley Improved chambers .014" shorter than the Ackley standard. Research turned up the true specifications.

Remington simply did the math and applied a datum line to the Ackley chamber along the 40 degree shoulder. So while they say the SAAMI chamber is .014" shorter it's not. The companies involved *did not* move the shoulder or the junction point of the shoulder and the neck.

Confusion comes from the change of the chamber drawings and gauges to the standard SAAMI method of measuring as apposed to the Ackley design. Ackley simply took a factory style Go gauge and shortened it by .004" to create his Go gauge. This meant that the gauge still had the factory shoulder angle (17 degree, 15 minute), not the new 40 degree shoulder.

SAAMI gauges do sport the 40 degree shoulder. Consequently, the datum point on the SAAMI gauge is .014" shorter than the junction point of the Ackley gauge. As discussed earlier 30-06 class cartridges use a datum line at the point along the shoulder that measures .375". This is the method that Remington, Nosler, and SAAMI have applied to the 280 Ackley Improved.

Look at the SAAMI drawing for the 280 AI where the headspace is called out from the .375 datum line, it's not the junction of the neck and shoulder. This datum line is .014" shorter than if you measured from the junction of the neck and shoulder in the Improved chamber, because it is at the point down the shoulder where it measures .375" in diameter.

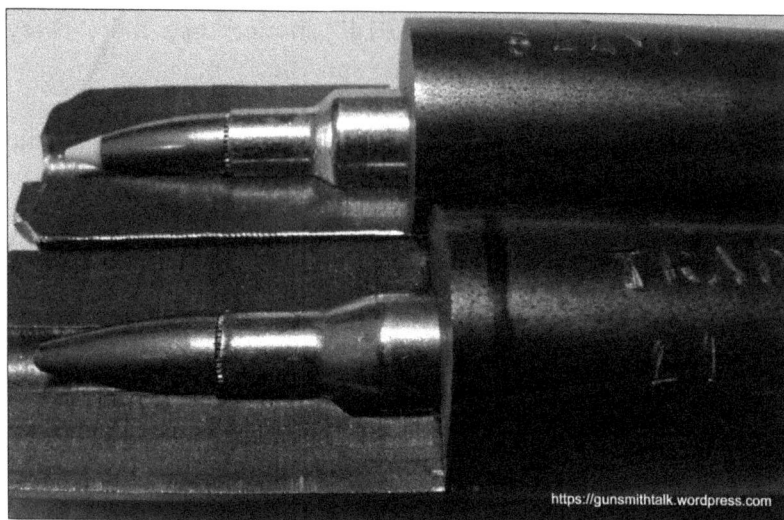

Above: How ammo interacts with the chamber.
Top is 280AI Nosler brass.
Bottom is 280 Remington factory.

Nosler, SAAMI, and indirectly Remington all site headspace as the reason for the change, unfortunately they did not fully explain the change, which caused controversy. Headspace was not the reason, it was simply to bring the cartridge into line with the SAAMI standard method of measuring headspace.

On the next page are pictured a set of chambers or case gauges that we made up to check empirically the measurements of the SAAMI and "Traditional" (Ackley) chambers for the 280 Ackley Improved. They were chambered using the same reamer, only the gauges differ.

The chamber gauges are marked as to which headspace gauge was used when they were chambered, so there can be no confusion. When they were finished the first thing we did was to switch the gauges between the two, according to the controversy there should have been a .014" difference. Actual results, zero difference.

These pictures are shown to help you visualize all the dimensional information given in the paragraphs above.

Here we have 280 Ackley Improved brass from Norma, they make the brass for Nosler. Note that there is no difference in how the cases protrude from our case gauges. The gauge on the right is chambered using the SAAMI headspace gauge. The gauge on the left is chambered using the "Traditional" Ackley headspace gauge.

I have had numerous inquiries about the details described here. All details have been checked and rechecked. Any reamers that may have varied from the current prints are now very old. In talking to the reamer makers, they have all been following the same standard now for many years. If in doubt, make sure your reamer was made 2006 or later.

In summary, if your gun is properly headspaced with the correct gauges there is no real difference between the SAAMI and the "Traditional" 280 Ackley chamber (the reamers are identical). So, you can still fireform using factory 280 Remington, or you can use the Nosler brass. If you have doubts just check your headspace with the correct gauges before you fire the next round.

If you are having headspace issues with Nosler brass the chances are that your gun is headspaced incorrectly. The previous statement is true simply because we used both gauges and with factory brass they fit the same as you have seen here. This is why it is important to understand the correct method of headspacing Ackley cartridges.

Appendix I

For a video about the 280 Ackley Improved headspace tests see this video on Youtube.
http://youtu.be/Vlskn2CE7-Y

For a video that explains the Ackley Improved headspace concepts for Traditional Ackley chambers see this Youtube video.
http://youtu.be/gStU24K0p8k

Appendix II, Ackley Improved Cartridges

Below is a chart of the most popular of Ackley Improved chamber dimensions.[16]

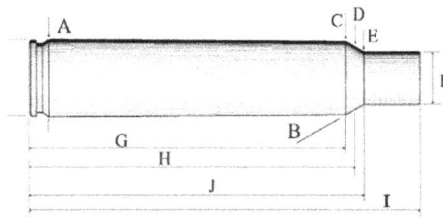

Cartridge	A	B	C	D	E	F	G	H	I	J	Trim
22-250 AI	.4722	40°	.455	.347	.257	.255	1.5375	1.6018	1.924	1.6555	1.910
223 AI	.376	40°	3.687	.330	.255	.254	1.4801	1.5032	1.772	1.5479	1.760
243 AI	.4722	40°	.4600	.400	.2783	.277	1.6849	1.7207	2.055	1.7932	1.710
244/6mm AI	.4742	40°	.455	.375	.278	.277	1.7665	1.8142	2.254	1.8720	2.240
250/3000 AI	.471	40°	.455	.347	.287	.286	1.5329	1.597	1.922	1.633	1.910
257 Roberts AI	.4722	40°	.455	.375	.292	.291	1.785	1.837	2.253	1.891	2.240
25-06 AI	.4722	40°	.455	.375	.292	.291	2.065	2.1127	2.502	2.1622	2.490
6.5-06 AI	.4722	40°	.455	.375	.298	.297	2.071	2.1187	2.502	2.1646	2.490
7x57 AI	.4745	40°	.455	.375	.323	.321	1.80	1.8256	2.253	2.878	2.540
30-06 AI	.473	40°	.454	.375	.340	.3395	2.00	2.0773	2.504	2.069	2.490
308 Win. AI	.4722	40°	.460	.400	.3462	.3442	1.632	1.6678	2.025	1.6999	2.015
8mm-06 AI	.4722	40°	.455	.375	.356	.355	2.00	2.0477	2.502	2.059	2.490
338-06 AI	.473	40°	.454	.420	.363	.362	2.00	2.0241	2.494	2.053	2.490
35 Whelen AI	.473	40°	.454	.400	.388	.387	2.00	2.0125	2.094	2.028	2.490
375 Whelen AI	.473	40°	.454		.397	.396	2.00		2.494	2.018	2.490

---

[16] Pocket Manual for Shooters and Reloaders, P.O. Ackley, 1964

About the Author…

Fred Zeglin has been building custom rifles for nearly 30 years and specializes in wildcat designs for his clients. He is currently the Firearms Technology Coordinator and the NRA Short Term Gunsmithing Program Coordinator for Flathead Community College in Kalispell, MT. He owns 4D Reamer Rentals Ltd. so he deals with more reamers and headspace gauges than any other gunsmith you will ever meet.

He has taught NRA Gunsmithing courses in Wildcat Cartridge Design at Murray State College in Oklahoma, Flathead Valley Community College in Montana and Trinidad State Junior College in Colorado. Fred also worked with AGI to create a Wildcat Cartridge lesson and Reloading instruction on DVD.

Fred has written articles for Precision Shooting Magazine, Guns and Ammo, and many others. He hosted an award winning podcast about gunsmithing at:
http://www.stitcher.com/podcast/gunsmithing-radio
Fred also writes a gunsmithing blog, that can be found at:
https://gunsmithtalk.wordpress.com

Andy Hill at Hawk Bullets, had this to say about Fred, "During the normal course of business we have gotten to know some gunsmiths with superb skills, artists crafting metal and wood into fine and functional firearms. Usually their ballistic knowledge is well rounded, but we believe one such gunsmith is quickly becoming a modern day P.O. Ackley. He is Fred Zeglin and he has done extensive development of a line of wildcat cartridges gaining popularity for their ballistic properties and low felt recoil." Fine praise from a craftsman of quality bullets.

This book is part of a series of gunsmith manuals that Fred is writing. Titles include: Understanding Headspace, Chambering for Ackley Cartridges, Relining Barrels, Glass Bedding Rifles for

Stability and Accuracy, and Chambering Rifle Barrels for Accuracy. With more to follow.

Look for other books in the:
 "Gunsmithing Student Handbook Series".

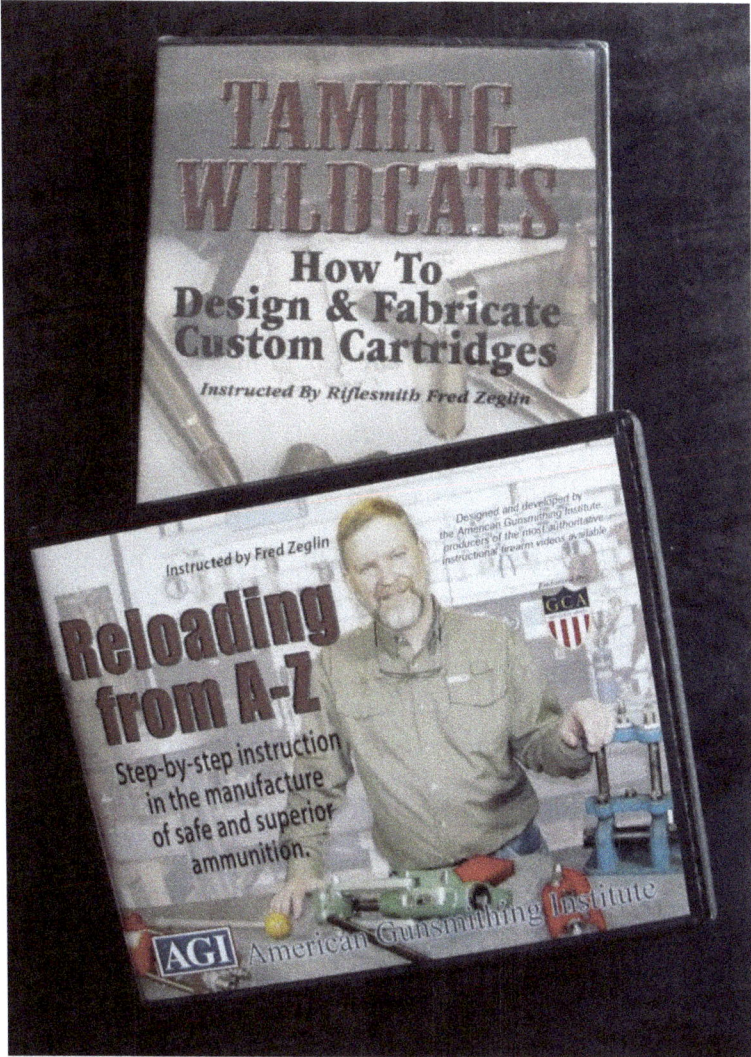

Video Courses Fred has done for AGI.

Hawk Reloading Manual

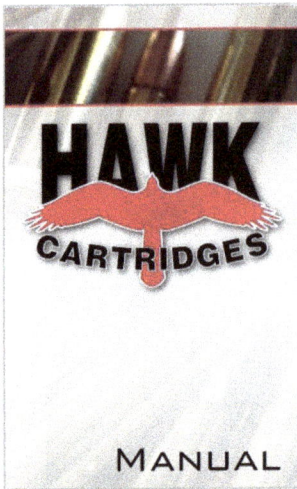

This hardback book contains 188 pages of stories, illustrations, anecdotes, instructions, and data.

Hawk Cartridges are unusual in wildcat circles in that, correctly headstamped brass is available for them. In partnership with Z-Hat Custom Inc., Quality Cartridge of Hollywood, NJ manufactures the brass as well as custom loaded ammunition.

Each cartridge covered in the book includes a dimensioned drawing. Contributions from Wayne van Zwoll, Michael Petrov, Dick Williams and Mike Brady are included. Pressure tested data is included for the majority of the load data and all loads are real world tested in firearms.

History of Hawk Cartridges is presented. This collection of data includes new material and new cartridges that were not included in the earlier electronic version of the manual. The intention is to provide information that time has shown to be valuable to shooters of Hawk Cartridges and for cartridge collectors. You can buy the Hawk Manual @: http://www.4-dproducts.com/

Can be purchased on Amazon.com
Hawk Reloading Manual

Wildcat Cartridges,
Reloader's Handbook of Wildcat Cartridge Design

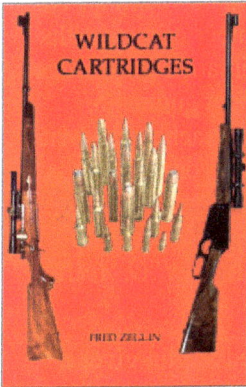

Wildcatting has been around almost as long as the metallic cartridge case. Wildcats have an air of mystery about them, no effort is made in these pages to diminish that mystique. Yet, you will find information here that is simply not available anywhere else. P.O. Ackley was the last Gunsmith to address the subject of wildcatting in depth. Over forty years later, Fred Zeglin, Master Rifle Builder and wildcatter has assembled in an easy to read, often humorous manual for anyone who loves guns, reloading, or wildcat cartridges.

History of wildcat cartridges is presented including many well known designers like P.O. Ackley, Jerry Gebby, and Charles Newton. The historical information provides an appropriate frame of reference for wildcatting. Nobody really wants to repeat something that has already been done. More recent wildcats are included along with reloading data and dimensions wherever possible.

Most valuable of all is the how-to information about making reamers and reloading dies. Fred supplies dimensions and instructions on how they are used to produce highly accurate reloading dies and chambers. Delivery times for such custom tools can delay a wildcat project by many months, knowing how to make your own dies can speed delivery of custom projects considerably.

Can be purchased on Amazon.com
Wildcat Cartridges,
Reloader's Handbook of Wildcat Cartridge Design

P.O. Ackley, America's Gunsmith

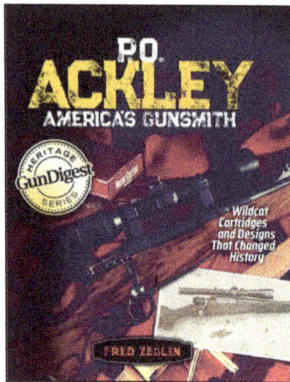

Parker Otto Ackley is arguably the most important gunsmith of the 20th century. He trained an incredible number of gunsmiths and shared a wealth of firearms knowledge along the way. The eminent gunsmith, ballistician, barrel maker, teacher and writer perhaps had more influence on modern shooting and firearms than any other single person. And now his life and works have been painstakingly detailed in *P.O. Ackley: America's Gunsmith.*

Writer and gunsmith Fred Zeglin gives a never-before-seen look at the humble man whose research thrust the firearms industry forward. From pushing rifle chambers to their limits and developing superior barrels to designing red-hot cartridges, readers will walk away with a new appreciation for Ackley's exploration and ideas. And his concepts on reloading, rifle accuracy, safety, cartridge choice, and wildcat use are just as relevant for today's "gun cranks" as they were in Ackley's heyday.

Zeglin also delivers the most complete collection of accurate dimensions, loading data (much of it with pressure data) and history for the lifetime of cartridges created by P.O. Ackley.

Most shooters today know him because of his "Ackley Improved" cartridge designs. But those cartridges are only the tip of the iceberg. *P.O. Ackley: America's Gunsmith* is the whole story.

Bonus: Full-color photo section and an exclusive never-before-printed article by P.O. Ackley.

You can buy P.O. Ackley, America's Gunsmith @: http://www.4drentals.com or, check out http://AckleyImproved.com where Fred continues to share new information and items that would not fit in the Ackley book.

www.ingramcontent.com/pod-product-compliance
Lightning Source LLC
Chambersburg PA
CBHW071100280326
41928CB00050B/2571